HELEN BRADLEY

AND MISS CARTER WORE PINK

SCENES FROM AN EDWARDIAN CHILDHOOD

JONATHAN CAPE THIRTY BEDFORD SQUARE LONDON

To Dear George with my love

FIRST PUBLISHED 1971
REPRINTED 1971, 1972, 1973
TEXT AND ILLUSTRATIONS © 1971 BY HELEN BRADLEY

JONATHAN CAPE LTD, 30 BEDFORD SQUARE, LONDON WCI

ISBN 0 224 00581 2

PRINTED AND BOUND IN GREAT BRITAIN
BY JARROLD & SONS LTD, NORWICH

I WAS BORN IN THE YEAR 1900 IN THE VILLAGE OF LEES, SITUATED BETWEEN OLDHAM and the nearby Yorkshire villages of Greenfield, Uppermill and Dobcross. Even then the village had lost the few farms it once had. The cotton mills had spread out from Oldham, and rows of little back-to-back houses for working people filled the once open spaces. Both my Grandfathers had owned businesses and even before I was born had built some of these houses which they let to good and trusted workers. My Father's Father bought a farm at South Shore, Blackpool, and built a nice house with plenty of room, because, he said, he wanted somewhere for his grandchildren to come for holidays; many were the happy holidays we spent there.

We lived in Lees in a tall Victorian house on the High Street. It had long narrow passages and steep stairs, and a large, warm kitchen with a good black coal range with two ovens: one we called the Bread Oven, and in the smaller one were cooked pies, puddings, etc. All our bread, cakes and biscuits were made at home by Mother or Sarah, who came to help when my brother George was a baby. As we grew older Annie Simpson came to help with the housework. On Tuesdays she "did" the bedrooms, singing lustily as she swept. She belonged to the Salvation Army in Oldham and always began with "Onward Christian Soldiers Going as to War", and when she saw George and me she would say, "Come along, children, join in," and away she would go again through all the verses, cheerfully banging about with her brushes and mops. Then we would sing "There is a Happy Land", and lots more lively hymns. We always knew when she was getting to the end of her work because she invariably finished off with "The Day Thou Gavest, Lord, is Ended". By the time she had done, it was afternoon, and on a dark winter's day "Darkness was falling" and it seemed, indeed, like the end of the day.

Alas, it was a sad day for us when poor Annie Simpson died. One afternoon when Mother paid her, she said in her cheerful voice, "Well, Missus, I guess I shan't be coming next week, but I'll see you in a fortnight." The following Tuesday afternoon Annie Simpson and her baby son were laid to rest in Leesfield Cemetery.

After Annie we had to put up with Mrs Murgatroyd. She had just lost her husband, and everyone who could afford to gave her employment. But she was not happy like Annie Simpson—and she brought Willie and Annie with her. George and I had lessons at home, so when Willie and Annie came they joined us. I never learnt anything on the dreadful mornings when they came because Willie Murgatroyd used to chew the blotting paper and push it in the inkwell or down my neck. It was so nice to see them go home and to have our dinner in peace. Afterwards we'd get ready to call for Grandma and go on our afternoon walk.

Grandma's house was only on the other side of the High Street and as in those days there were only horses plodding slowly by with their lorry-loads of bales of cotton we could run across to see her without much fear of accident. Grandfather, our Mother's Father, had died, and with Grandma lived Aunt Mary (the eldest Aunt), Aunt Frances and pretty Aunt Charlotte. Their house was an old stone one, with a long low room at the top known as the Loom House. Two large looms were always in use there. Maggie Knott, who was very old, came to weave the cotton or linen sheets on one. Aunt Mary had the other loom, and in her spare time wove yards of woollen cloth for winter coats, or fine pieces for frocks, just as Mother or the Aunts required them.

Our afternoon walk was always the same. First, we called for Grandma and the Aunts. Farther along the High Street lived Miss Carter (who wore Pink). She was always ready and waiting. Next door lived Mrs Maitland and Emily, but we did not call for them because Mrs Maitland was never sure how she would be feeling and she might have to lie down for a little while if her head wasn't too good. George and I didn't like having her come with us, because, as Grandma said, she had been cast down ever since the death of her dear husband Samuel. But for the sake of Emily, who was so sweet and patient, we had to be nice to her Mother; otherwise Emily would never have been allowed out.

As we all walked along Spring Lane towards the cemetery, Miss Carter walked in the midst of the ladies because she always had such thrilling news about Mr Taylor (the Bank Manager). She called Mother "Jane" and she would stand still in the middle of the lane, close her eyes, and clasp her hands and say, "Oh Jane, when we left you yesterday, do you know what he did, he gently took my arm and I really thought he was going to propose, when we saw Mrs Hope-Ainsworth with Nellie and Bertie crossing over to speak to us. I know I ought to have asked them in and offered tea, but I came over quite faint." And so, slowly, we would approach the cemetery with its wide path and rows of seats filled with more friends. Mary Ellen, John Henry's wife, would be keeping a place next to her for Grandma, while Florrie, John Sam'els wife, would be anxious to hear the latest about Mr Taylor, but everyone had to be careful what they said to Florrie because she was a dreadful gossip.

There was a new curate at Leesfield called Mr Albert Green. All the ladies thought him very handsome, and often in the afternoons he would stroll along the path and have a word with everyone. Aunt Frances, who was more strict about lessons than Mother, would take George and me by the hand and we would spell out the names on the gravestones. Mr Green would walk along with us — but only when Aunt Charlotte was there.

Aunt Frances and Mother were sure he liked her very much. He would stare at her and she would lower her eyes and turn bright pink. He would often walk back with us as far as the Church, and would manage to say something special to her — it must have been nice because it made her look at him and smile. As the evenings lengthened she took to calling on us to ask if she could take George and me and the dogs, Gyp and Barney, for a walk before bedtime.

They were lovely walks along Spring Lane because she let us run and jump instead of walking sedately behind. Aunt Charlotte always looked surprised when she saw the Rev. Albert Green strolling towards us. "Good evening," she would say. "This is a nice surprise," and she would look so pretty in her spotted muslin gown and wide leghorn hat, and so happy.

Soon the Rev. Albert Green started to call on Grandma. It was discovered that he sang, so he was asked to our Saturday Evenings when everyone sang or played an instrument. Mother played the piano and Father the violin, and Aunt Mary's lovely contralto voice gave them a chance to sing many of the Victorian party songs. George and I were allowed to stay up until it was time to sing "Excelsior". When it came to the words "There was a banner with a strange device, Excelsior — Excel-si-or", we joined in with gusto. Then it was time for bed.

I would lie awake listening to Mother singing and Father playing. Then Mr Taylor would arrive. With Mr Green singing tenor and Mr Taylor with his rich baritone, they would start to sing parts of the *Messiah*, and to the beautiful, rich sound of "Worthy is the Lamb" I would fall asleep. Soon the Rev. Albert forgot his shyness and sang "Drink to me only with thine eyes" and "Only to thee, my love" in his thin high voice. He always stood with his hand on his heart looking at Aunt Charlotte who always looked at the carpet and grew pink. They were delightful evenings which ended with the handing round of plates of roast beef sandwiches and cups of China tea or Sandow's Cocoa.

The first holiday of the year was at Easter, when we all went to visit Grandpa at Blackpool. Everyone met at Mumps Station with plenty of time to spare, because Father had to see that all the luggage was safely in the guard's van. Not only had he our luggage to see to, but all the trunks and suitcases that Grandma, the Aunts, Miss Carter and Mrs Maitland and Emily were taking with them. Mr Taylor, who was coming too, helped him. There were mountains of luggage, bundles of umbrellas and parasols, our buckets and spades, as well as the dogs, Gyp and Barney, and two wicker baskets with the cats,

Mother, George and I with the dogs Gyp and Barney. Although Mother was tall, she only took size two-and-a-half shoes.

Aunt Frances, Aunt Charlotte and Aunt Mary. Aunt Frances was small and dark and took size two shoes, Aunt Charlotte, small and delicate and fair, took size two-and-a-half shoes and Aunt Mary, more sturdy, took size three.

Martha and Nelson, inside.

Grandma, the Aunts, Miss Carter (who wore Pink), Mrs Maitland and Emily always took a house in Lytham Road, and Mr Taylor (the Bank Manager) had lodgings a few doors away. He was so kind, so courteous to all the ladies, dividing his attentions between each in turn. Dear Mr Taylor was a widower, now considered out of mourning for his wife — "And it's possible", said Mother one morning, "that he is looking out for a new wife." Everyone was certain that eventually he would ask Miss Carter to marry him, because she had Private Means; but in the spring of 1907 he was still dividing his attentions between Aunt Frances, Aunt Charlotte and Miss Carter.

Mother, George and I usually stayed at Blackpool until a fortnight before Whitsuntide. They were happy days, with lessons on the beach every morning, and no Friday evening visits from Mr Thornley, the teacher who came to examine me on my spelling. He was so big, so fierce and had such bristling whiskers that I was afraid of him, so whenever he asked me to spell "mouse" I always forgot how to. He would look at me and shake his head and say, "Dear, dear, doesn't the child learn anything?"

When the holidays were over and we had to return home to Lees, there was much talk and thought about the New Clothes. We had to have everything new and ready for Whitsuntide. If we met friends on our afternoon walks, clothes were not mentioned. Miss Carter pretended to be uninterested, but she would take to calling on Grandma whenever she thought we were all together, hoping to catch Mother and the Aunts trimming their new hats or trying on dresses. She longed to know what colours they would choose, or whether they were going to bring out their last year's leghorns to be retrimmed. What a rush it was when we heard a knock at the door! Everything had to be gathered up and hidden. And how everyone hoped for a fine day for the Whit Walks! Whit Walks are long processions through the streets that take place every Whitsuntide. Everybody joins in, all dressed in their new clothes. I can't remember it ever raining on the Whit Walks, and even the poorest child had a new white frock to walk in the processions.

After Whitsuntide we packed up again and all went back to Blackpool to spend the long summer days on the beach or going for walks along The Lanes. So the year passed. We would be home in the autumn to go on our last picnics and The Mothers' Union Outing, and as the winter nights drew towards Christmas there was much sewing of patchwork quilts, and getting ready for the Christmas Bazaar. Then came the School Treat, which George and I didn't really enjoy because Mr Thornley pretended to be Father Christmas, and in spite of his bristling side whiskers and beard whitened with flour, I felt afraid he would demand that I spelled "mouse" before he would give me an orange.

It was nice when we got home and hung up our stockings, for it would be "Christmas Day In The Morning", and all the Bells would Ring, and everyone sang "Christians Awake". George and I would have our Orange and Apple, our bright new Penny, a new Threepenny Piece, and a piece of coal for luck. The sky would be blue and the snow would be Deep and Crisp and Even. George and I would be warmly wrapped up and go in the trap with Father down to the warehouse and stables, because even though it was Christmas the other horses had to be fed.

And so the years went by. The happy years of childhood. By the time I was ten we had to go to school and it was goodbye to our afternoon walks and listening to the doings of Miss Carter, Mr Taylor, Mrs Maitland and Emily. Mr Green, the new curate, had long since left to go to Darkest Africa — and, "Oh dear," said Aunt Charlotte, "he's sure to be eaten by a lion." It was goodbye to our world of grown-ups into an astonishing world of lots of children and books, books which brought to me the whole world. But the memories of the afternoon walks along Spring Lane, and Mother in her white spotted muslin dress, and the pretty Aunts all with their befrilled parasols — those memories will be always there.

THE FIRST early days of spring – when it became light enough for the children to play out after tea, and Mother, Aunt Frances and Aunt Mary, George and I (and the dogs Gyp and Barney) could go for a walk before it was time for bed. Aunt Mary stopped to talk to Sarah Ann Thompson, who complained that now that summer and the light nights were coming the children would chalk all over her clean flags and make a noise outside her window. "Never mind, Sarah Ann," said Mother. "Children are children for such a little while."

IT WAS the time of half-mourning for Grandfather (my Mother's Father) and a lovely warm day, which enabled Mother and Aunt Frances to wear their muslins with lavender silk slips underneath. Everyone brought spring flowers to the cemetery and George and I looked at our favourite angel whilst Mother and the Aunts made Grandfather's grave look gay with flowers. Miss Carter (who wore Pink) had a large grave to keep nice, for both her parents and brother were dead. Mrs Maitland and Emily talked to Mr Taylor (the Bank Manager). After everything was tidy, we all walked round the paths, meeting friends—then came back to Grandma, who was sitting talking to Mary Ellen, John Henry's wife.

MOTHER, George and I and Gyp and Barney had called for Grandma and the Aunts and Miss Carter to ask if they would like to go on the tram to Chadwick's Hat Shop in the town. Mother didn't find a hat to suit her but Aunt Mary brought a new toque. Coming home along Union Street we saw a dreadful mill fire. It had just begun at the top of the building and it horrified us to see the red glow going downwards from floor to floor. Mr Taylor who had walked along to meet us took off his shiny tall hat and black frock coat which he handed to Miss Carter. He was going to help. "Oh, how brave you are," cried Aunt Charlotte. "We'll stay with you." But Mother thought it wisest to take Grandma, George and me (and the dogs) home.

"PLEASE Marion, stop Willie Murgatroyd from fighting George"…but Marion and Susan Verney were too busy playing at being grown-up ladies. George and I had been asked to play with Marion and her little sister in their back garden, and we were having a beautiful Dolls' Tea Party when Willie and Annie Murgatroyd arrived. He didn't like dolls or playing at being Father, so he chased George until George escaped into the outside toilet and locked the door. But when it came time to go home George couldn't unlock the door and had to stay until Marion's Father came home and got him out.

ON THE First of May the Pot Market came to Lees. Mother, George and I and the dogs, Gyp and Barney, called for Grandma and the Aunts to come and see if there was anything new. Aunt Mary was delighted and said they needed some new basins. Who should they meet but Miss Carter. "What a pity", said Aunt Frances and Aunt Charlotte, "dear Mr Taylor (the Bank Manager) isn't here to walk back with us." "But", said Mother, "I can see him coming. He's just by the lamp post putting his tie straight." George and I could see some May Queens coming along. Some naughty boys saw them also and started to fight. We saw Willie and Annie Murgatroyd dash across the square to join in.

"It's going to be a beautiful sunny evening when we get to Blackpool," said Mother, and we could see the drab towns being left behind and the real country beginning with lush pastures filled with cows and lots of big trees. Father, Mother, George and I and the dogs, Gyp and Barney, Grandma and the three Aunts were in a second-class compartment, chatting away and planning all the outings we were going to have when we got to Blackpool. Mr Taylor had to travel first class along with Miss Carter and Mrs Maitland and Emily. Grandma, the Aunts, Miss Carter, Mrs Maitland and Emily took a house in Lytham Road, while Mr Taylor had lodgings a few doors away, to be near so as to look after the ladies. Father, Mother, George and I and the dogs and cats stayed with Grandpa and had a lovely time.

"QUICKLY, children, the tide is coming in," called Mother, while Father crossly looked at his watch — it was time for the band to start on the pier and he wanted to get there. I didn't want to leave the sands — my new blue kite was just beginning to fly beautifully and besides, George, who was standing in the water, wanted to try. But Mother said perhaps tomorrow would be a lovely windy day. Aunt Mary and Grandma were already walking towards the steps while Aunt Frances and Aunt Charlotte were waiting to tell Mother that they had seen Mr Taylor take Miss Carter's arm.

WALKING along Watsons Lane, Blackpool, during a shower, we met some gipsies camping by the roadside. Mother, George and I stopped to admire a tiny gipsy baby whose mother was little more than a girl. She held him out to Mother saying, "Missus, would you like him? He's called Ralph and he's only five days old. I don't want him, we have plenty of children." "My dear," said Mother, "he's beautiful, and just think how proud you'll be of him some day." The girl let me hold him before she popped him in a box of hay with four fat puppies. "Well," said Mother when she told the Aunts and Miss Carter, "that's one way of keeping babies warm and snug." "Disgusting," said Mr Taylor.

13

"COME children, the shadows are beginning to lengthen and Grandpa is waiting with Prince."
And by the time we arrived home it would be bedtime for George and me. It was one of our
last outings, for in a few more days we would be back in Lees. Before setting off with Grandpa
and the wagonette we saw the cows come to the pond for a drink before going to be milked. Even Miss
Carter said it was one of the happiest days of the holiday.

"Look who's coming to call on us," cried Aunt Frances. "It's Miss Carter and behind her is Mr Taylor and they're bowing to the Hope-Ainsworths in their carriage. Bertie's driving, and I bet they turn round and call also." "Quick," said Mother, "move Aunt Charlotte's party dress in the other room. It's turning out beautifully and they're bound to copy it." "Nellie Bly," said Grandma, "gather up the bobbins of cotton, and George, pick up the pins. I'll pretend to be fast asleep, and girls, don't forget to take off your aprons." Nellie Bly was my nickname, after the girl in the rhyme: "Nellie Bly caught a fly,/Tied it to a string./ Let it out to fly about,/But couldn't get it in./Oh, Nellie! Oh, Nellie!"

IT WAS a warm day when we met in Manchester. Mother, George and I, Grandma and the two Aunts had just arrived outside the Royal Infirmary on Piccadilly when Miss Carter arrived with Mr Taylor. Everyone thought it so kind of him to accompany us to Affleck & Brown's to buy a carpet. George and I would have loved to stay with the pigeons, but the shopping had to be done. We did stop to buy some delicious Ashton-Moss celery, though, and Grandma bought some daffodils. Miss Carter lingered near the roses, but Mr Taylor gave all his attention to Grandma. There was a man lying on a bench and a letter boy called to a nurse, "Please come, I'm sure he's dead." We hurried away.

O N NICE summer evenings we walked through the park on our way home from having tea with Great-Aunt Buckley, who lived in a dark brown house on Greengate Street. George and I had been very good so Aunt Charlotte and Aunt Frances took us for a sail on the launch, which was quite a thrill. It took us past a little island where all the ducks were getting ready to roost for the night. As we got nearer the landing-stage we could see Grandma, Mother and Aunt Mary. Aunt Mary was holding the dogs Gyp and Barney, who barked when they saw us. Miss Carter (who wore Pink) and Mr Taylor (the Bank Manager) were walking back with us and would stay to supper at Grandma's while George and I went home to bed.

17

WE ALL went to the Fair at Daisy Nook, held every Whit Saturday. It had been a lovely afternoon, but George and I and even the dogs were growing tired. But George pleaded, "Can I have just one more ride on the roundabout?" Mother said no, but Grandma said, "Just let him learn that even a little boy can have too much of a good thing!" So George spent his last halfpenny and we saw him turning pale green. He was in deep disgrace and had to walk behind Mother, Grandma and the three Aunts. I held his hand as we walked home because he said, "All the world is going round and round."

ONE fine summer's day, Grandpa gave us a treat. We all went to Tarporley Races. Even Miss Carter came, and so did Mr Taylor. There we met Mrs Hope-Ainsworth with Bertie and Nellie, a dreadful girl who spent her time listening to other people's conversation. Then she would tell her Mother, especially if she thought any of the ladies of Lees fancied their Bertie. We only saw one race because Fanny and Prince thought they ought to join in, which quite frightened Mother, Grandma and the Aunts. There were lots of drunken men and we saw one man running away with a bag of money. Even Mr Taylor gave chase, shouting, "Stop thief."

"THE Day Thou gavest, Lord, is ended", sang the ladies of the Leesfield Mothers' Union at the end of their outing to Rostherne Mere in Cheshire. It had been a beautiful day with a good tea of home-cured ham and home-made bread and cakes in plenty. George and I gathered flowers to take back and it seemed a pity to see Mrs Maitland weeping after one had had such a good time. I heard Grandma remark that she was just silly and sentimental, and it was time she stopped feeling sorry for herself. Her husband had been dead at least five years and she was always curbing poor Emily who would never have a chance if her Mother didn't pull herself together.

GOING home after the Leesfield Mothers' Union treat. Everyone was climbing into the wagonette, and the Vicar made sure all the children were safely gathered together. Father brought Fanny and the dog-cart to get us home. George and I were going to sleep already, and Aunt Charlotte was taking *such* a long time to say "good night" to the Rev. Albert Green, the new and handsome curate. Aunt Frances whispered to Aunt Mary that Charlotte had blushed, and did she think there was anything in it. Mrs Hope-Ainsworth bowed to Miss Carter (who wore Pink) and offered her a lift, and said that she would see that Aunt Edith was taken safely home to Plymouth Grove, Manchester. Nellie Hope-Ainsworth was still listening to people talking so she could tell tales to her mother.

21

ONE year we went to watch the parade in aid of the New Royal Infirmary. It was a wonderful sight. The Oldham Brass Band headed the procession, and next came the Mayor and Mayoress in their carriage. "Look George, there's a beautiful Queen and Red Riding Hood, and look at Father giving a whole shilling to that funny man" (much to the wonder of those poor little children who are asking him for a penny). But I was sure I heard a Moo, although Mother said I was being foolish, they would not let bulls out while the parade was on. But they did.

22

OH, LOOK what has happened! Those bulls did get loose. They headed towards the people watching the parade, who rushed across the road to safety. Father quickly shepherded Mother, George and me, Grandma and the Aunts into a shop. Miss Carter and Mr Taylor were horrified to see Willie Murgatroyd become very sick. "Whatever have you been eating?" cried his Mother, who felt very annoyed, and to make matters worse, Annie cried at the top of her voice. The Hope-Ainsworths hurriedly moved to the far end of the picture out of Willie's way. He quite spoiled our day. Mother begged Father to take us home in case he was beginning with something...

23

"GOODBYE, Mary Ellen, goodbye," sighed Grandma, for Mary Ellen, John Henry's wife, had been Grandma's oldest friend and all through the long years they had faced joys and sorrows together. But through the winter Mary Ellen had gently and peacefully slipped away to her long rest. Aunt Frances turned to Mr Taylor to ask him if he would tell Miss Carter and Mother that we must hurry to the schoolroom to start to prepare Tea. Everyone helped to make it the sort of Tea that Mary Ellen would have been proud of.

"OH," SAID Mother, going very stiff, "it's a mouse!" George and I saw it first, nibbling away at a piece of bread. "Oh dear," cried Grandma, "there's another, sitting looking at me!" "I think, Jane," said Aunt Mary, "you'd better get your cottage loaf and I'll get the muffins and we'll go." When Den Lane Mill was burned down there was no work (or money) for Bob Hulme and his sister Alice, so their Mother turned her cottage into a Bread Shop. She and Alice baked bread and muffins (bread dough rolled out thin and baked on the oven bottom on a bakestone). They were crisp and delicious, especially eaten hot, pulled open and a lump of fresh farm butter popped inside. We always bought a cottage loaf on Tuesdays because our own home-made bread was still warm.

OING home through Alexandra Park on a winter evening. George and I, Mother, Grandma and the dogs had gone to meet Aunt Frances and Aunt Charlotte in the park. They had already met Miss Carter, and the three ladies were skating along when they saw Mr Taylor. "How kind dear Mr Taylor is," said Mother to Grandma. "But look, isn't that the Reverend Albert Green walking across the ice towards Charlotte—she is turning towards him. I wonder if anything will come of it." But George and I had something much more interesting to think about; all the ducks came across the ice asking for food, all the Japanese lanterns were lit, and everything looked like Fairyland. 27

UNCLE John's wedding was in a strange church on a cold winter's day. Mother looked lovely in blue, and Father had to carry George because at that time he wasn't big enough to walk. Aunt Frances and Aunt Mary were the bridesmaids in claret-red velvet trimmed with white fur. The best man was James Alfred, who had a secret passion for Aunt Frances. As soon as he got the chance he slipped out round the back and Aunt Frances slipped out of the front where they met by a gravestone. "Oh Frances," he said, taking her hand, "will you become…" but his Mother had seen him and before he could finish the sentence she called, "James Alfred, come here." So they waited and waited until Aunt Frances was fifty-two and Alfred was sixty, and then they were able to marry.

"COME along, children," said Mother, "it's too cold to stand about"…but, oh, the smell of Janey Mills cooking her fish and chips made George and me hungry. The evening was clear, cold and frosty, and we were on our way home from having tea with Grandma and the Aunts. Aunt Frances and Aunt Mary decided to walk part of the way with us. We met Miss Carter (who wore Pink), who was about to call on them, and behind her was Mr Taylor (the Bank Manager). It was no use asking for a pennyworth of chips with everyone laughing and talking, so we walked behind with Gyp and Barney, our dogs, and dreamed of bread with milk for supper.

"Oh GEORGE, look, Father Christmas isn't really Father Christmas but Mr Thornley." How sad we felt when we saw him standing at the schoolroom door shouting at the top of his voice, "Fetch my cane, Willie Murgatroyd, and get off the table, Sam Wilkins." It was a dreadful school party. Two of the teachers were ill, so Aunt Frances asked Mother to help and bring us along (also Gyp and Barney). But we couldn't stop Willie Murgatroyd and Sam Wilkins from fighting, and Annie urged them on. One little girl came to Mother and said, "Please, Miss, our Billy's wet his pants and I feel sick." "Frances," called Mother, "what do we do with her, she may be beginning with something..."

"OH COME All Ye Faithful" played the Salvation Army Band on the afternoon of Christmas Eve. It was a great treat for George and me to be taken into Oldham Market to listen and sing with it, but it had started snowing so Mother only let us have a quick look round the Market then took us back home by tram because neither Grandma nor the Aunts had umbrellas. Miss Carter (who wore Pink) came back with us and we all had tea at Grandma's. Then George and I hung up our stockings. We knew what would be in them—an Orange, an Apple, a new shiny Penny, a new Three-penny Piece and a piece of coal for Luck.

31